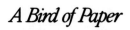

A Bird of Paper

for Elias L. Rivers

Un pàjaro
de papel.

boullata 81

A Bird
of Paper

POEMS OF
VICENTE ALEIXANDRE

Translated from the Spanish by

Willis Barnstone
David Garrison

INTERNATIONAL POETRY SERIES
BYBLOS EDITIONS
VOLUME VI

Ohio University Press
Athens, Ohio

Originally published as Volume VI of the Byblos Editions, International Poetry Forum, in a limited edition of two hundred copies.

The type is set in Alphatype Griffo Italic, composed by Davis & Warde, Inc. Designed by Thomas C. Pears III.

Publication of the Byblos Edition was made possible in part by grants from the Research Council and the Liberal Arts Faculty Research Committee of Wright State University.

First printing by Ohio University Press 1982.

ISBN 0-8214-0661-2 cloth
ISBN 0-8214-0662-0 paper

Library of Congress Catalog Card Number 82-80388

Foreword

This is the sixth book in the International Poetry Forum's Byblos Series. The first was Marco Antonio Montes de Oca's THE HEART OF THE FLUTE translated by Laura Villaseñor with an introduction by Octavio Paz. The second was Artur Lundkvist's AGADIR translated and with an introduction by William Jay Smith and Leif Sjöberg. Yannis Ritsos' SUBTERRANEAN HORSES in a translation by Minas Savvas and with an introduction by Vassilis Vassilikos was the third selection. The fourth and fifth were Bulgarian selections published simultaneously: Lyubomir Levchev's THE MYSTERIOUS MAN translated by Vladimir Phillipov, and Cornelia Bozhilova's translation of Bozhidar Bozhilov's AMERICAN PAGES. The present volume is in the same tradition of providing the best translations of some of the most significant poets in the world for an audience that would not otherwise be able to read them. A BIRD OF PAPER has the additional distinction of being the result of close collaboration between the Nobel Laureate Vicente Aleixandre and his friends and translators, Willis Barnstone and David Garrison.

Samuel Hazo
President and Director
International Poetry Forum

CONTENTS

Frontispiece by Kamal Boullata
Title Poem:

      Vida (from La destrucción o el amor*)* 4

      Life (from Destruction or Love*)*   5

An Introduction to the Poetry of Vicente Aleixandre   6

Poet's Preface   11

From Surroundings / Ambito (1928)
Adolescence / Adolescencia   12

From Swords Like Lips / Espadas como labios (1932)
My Voice / Mi voz   13
Now It is Late / Ya es tarde   14
Silence / Silencio   15
Love Poem / Poema de amor   16
Always / Siempre   18
Instant / Instante   19
Whiteness / Blancura   20

From Destruction or Love / La destrucción o el amor (1935)
Suspended Heart / Corazón en suspenso   21
To Death / A la muerte   22
Cobra / Cobra   24

From The World by Itself / Mundo a solas (finished in 1936
      but unpublished until 1950)
Inhuman World / Mundo inhumano   26

From Shadow of Paradise / Sombra del Paraíso (1944)
The Poet / El poeta   28
The Body and the Soul / El cuerpo y el alma   30
You Almost Loved Me / Casi me amabas   31

1

The Immortals / Los Inmortales
      I. Rain / La lluvia   33
      II. Sun / El Sol   34
      III. Word / La palabra   35
      IV. Earth / La tierra   36
      V. Fire / El fuego   37
      VI. Air / El aire   38
      VII. Sea / El mar   39
My Father (fragment) / Padre mío   40
From Final Birth / Nacimiento último (1953)
Epitaph / Epitafio   41
To Fray Luis de León / A Fray Luis de León   42
To Don Luis de Góngora / A Don Luis de Góngora   43

From The Story of the Heart / Historia del corazón (1954)
Final Shadow / Sombra final   44
In the Square / En la plaza   45
The Dream / El sueño   47

From Various Poems / Poemas varios (1927-1967; published
      in volumes of Aleixandre's complete works)
The Mirror / El espejo   48
My Night / Noche mía   50

From Poems of Consummation / Poemas de la consumación
      (1968)
The Years / Los años   51
Vision of Youth from Other Years / Visión juvenil desde otros años   52
A Few Words / Unas pocas palabras   53
At Last / Por fin   54
Doesn't Know / No lo conoce   55
Limits and Mirror / Límites y espejo   56
Face Behind the Glass (The Old Man's Gaze) / Rostro tras el
      cristal (Mirada del viejo)   59
You Wait / Esperas   60
Raining / Llueve   61

The Poet Remembers His Life / El poeta se acuerda de su vida   62
Night Cave / Cueva de noche   63
Yesterday / Ayer   64
Posthumous Kiss / Beso Póstumo   65
The Limit / El Límite   66
Impure Dream / Sueño impuro   67
Permanence / Permanencia   68
Another Truth / Otra verdad   69
Forgetting / El olvido   70
Aliki / Aliki*   71

Notes:
    About the poet   73
    About the translators   74
    About the Spanish texts and the translations   75

*An encuentro *about Aliki Barnstone*

Vida

Un pájaro de papel en el pecho
dice que el tiempo de los besos no ha llegado;
vivir, vivir, el sol cruje invisible,
besos o pájaros, tarde o pronto o nunca.
Para morir basta un ruidillo,
el de otro corazón al callarse,
o ese regazo ajeno que en la tierra
es un navío dorado para los pelos rubios.
Cabeza dolorida, sienes de oro, sol que va a ponerse;
juncos de verde sangre que ahora nace,
sueño apoyado en ti calor o vida.

by Vicente Aleixandre

Life

A bird of paper in my chest
says the time of kisses hasn't come.
To live, live, the sun crackles invisibly,
kisses or birds, late or soon or never.
To die a tiny noise will do,
as when another heart is silenced,
or that foreign lap on the earth
that is a gold ship for blond hairs.
Aching head, its gold temples, sun about to set,
here darkly I dream a river,
reeds of green blood being born,
I dream leaning on you, heat or life.

Translated by Willis Barnstone

An Introduction to the Poetry of Vicente Aleixandre

Vicente Aleixandre, winner of the 1977 Nobel Prize for Literature, was born in Seville in 1898. Along with Rafael Alberti, Dámaso Alonso and Jorge Guillén, he is one of the last living poets of Spain's Generation of 1927, which included Federico García Lorca, Luis Cernuda, Pedro Salinas, Gerardo Diego and others. Although all these poets have highly distinctive voices, their lives and work manifest certain shared ideals. They held a special esteem for the baroque craftsman of language, Luis de Góngora, who had in large part been forgotten until their revival of interest in his work. The year 1927 marked the third centenary of Góngora's death, and their homage to him in that year gave the group its name. Aleixandre wrote a sonnet in honor of Góngora and a short prose poem about him. But he paid an even more personal tribute: the color, the extravagant metaphors and the elaborate rhetorical devices of many of his poems recall the baroque poet.

Aleixandre's early work is largely surrealistic, but not in any doctrinaire sense, for he has never accepted the notion of automatic writing. In many of these poems we may not understand everything at the literal level, for Aleixandre's imagery speaks to us through the logic of dreams and the unconscious. In Swords Like Lips (Espadas como labios) *and* Destruction or Love (La destrucción o el amor) *the poet achieves some of his greatest power in short, dense, enigmatic pieces such as "Life" (Vida"). This poem shows the fundamental oppositions in the imagery and thought of Aleixandre, oppositions between desire and fulfillment, sunlight and shadow, life and death. In the first four verses the poet uses explosive alliteration and repetition to emphasize the images of desire, life and light:*

> *A bird of paper in my chest*
> *says the time of kisses hasn't come.*
> *To live, live, the sun crackles invisibly,*
> *kisses or birds, late or soon or never.*

> *Un pájaro de papel en el pecho*
> *dice que el tiempo de los besos no ha llegado;*
> *vivir, vivir, el sol cruje invisible,*
> *besos o pájaros, tarde o pronto o nunca.*

After these incantatory lines, the very short, simple verse

> *To die a tiny noise will do*

> *Para morir basta un ruidillo*

has the irony and deceptively mundane quality of Emily Dickinson's

> *The Dying need but little, Dear,*
> *A Glass of Water's all . . .*

The poem, "Life," and the title of the book from which it comes, Destruction or Love, *reveal a basic metaphorical equation between love and death. In his address upon entering the Spanish Royal Academy, Aleixandre spoke of these themes as "two great ideas that the poet rarely separates from the unity of their root . . . two faces of the same ultimate, total reality." Or, as he said in a letter to Dámaso Alonso, love is a semblance, an image of man's desire for union with the cosmos. It is the only image of this desire that is possible in life, for real unification occurs only in "the true amorous destruction — death."*

The World by Itself (Mundo a solas) *was completed in 1936 shortly before the outbreak of the Spanish Civil War. Here Aleixandre foresees the imminent tragedy. The most pessimistic of his books,* The World by Itself, *is filled with images of grief and foreboding. Human beings are portrayed as weakened, overcome by the pain of existence, constantly forced to doubt the most ordinary realities. In fact the first poem is entitled, "Man Does Not Exist" ("No existe el hombre"), and this idea is echoed throughout the book. In the poem, "Inhuman World" ("Mundo inhumano") he says:*

Man is remote. High wall of blood.
Man deafly screams out his forest heart.
His dripping blood, his stone sadness.

El hombre está lejos. Alta pared de sangre.
El hombre grita sordo su corazón de bosque.
Su gotear de sangre, su pesada tristeza.

The World by Itself *reflects a transition between the early surrealism and the cosmic vision of* Shadow of Paradise (Sombra del Paraíso), *Aleixandre's most famous book.* Shadow of Paradise *is a clear resounding statement of his central poetic insight. He calls it "a song about the dawn of the world as seen by people today, a canticle of light from the consciousness of darkness." The poet envisions not one but many kinds of paradise—nature before the advent of human beings, moments of harmony and peace, the innocence of youth, the happiness of love. Although the book maintains much of the pessimism of* The World by Itself, *the life force in it is re-invigorated. This force is often described as a primal sexual energy that is alternately caged and released. In "You Almost Loved Me" (Casi me amabas"), an ambivalent reflection on a past love affair, the lovers are part of nature itself. They meet and love like elemental forces of the universe. The man is associated with land: he emerges from "a dark consciousness of earth." The woman, like Venus, rises from the ocean on a shell. This mixture of mythological allusion and exuberant orchestration of colors and cosmic images recalls the poetry of Góngora:*

An ocean depth surrounded you.
An unbroken mother-of-pearl shell beneath your foot
tenders you like the last drop of seafoam.
Almost . . . , you almost loved me.

Why did you turn your eyes away, virgin from the core of
        the world?
Why, this spring afternoon,

do you place moon coldness over daylight
and like a disc of nightless chastity
race roseate through inviolate blue?

Un fondo marino te rodeaba.
Una concha de nácar intacta bajo tu pie, te ofrece
a ti como la última gota de una espuma marina.
Casi . . . , casi me amabas.

¿Por qué viraste los ojos, virgen de las entrañas del mundo
que esta tarde de primavera
pones frialdad de luna sobre la luz del día
y como un disco de castidad sin noche,
huyes rosada por un azul virgíneo?

While Shadow of Paradise *illuminates our place and condition within the cosmos, Aleixandre's next few books focus on earthly ventures.* The Story of the Heart (Historia del corazón) *is a book about the complexity of love.* "The Dream" ("El sueño"), *from that collection, expresses the sadness of a failure of love. It begins at a moment of recognition:*

There are moments of loneliness
when the heart knows dumbly that it doesn't love.

Hay momentos de soledad
en que el corazón reconoce, atónito, que no ama.

It ends as the speaker's new awareness leads him, like the character in "The Circular Ruins" of Borges, to feel that his very existence is an illusion:

And the only sound is someone's slow breathing,
that woman over there, serene, beautiful, sleeping
and dreaming that you don't love her, and you are her dream.

Y solo suena el pausado respiro de alguien,
de aquella que allí, serena, bellísima, duerme
y sueña que no la quieres, y tú eres su sueño.

Aleixandre's later books are among his most important. Poems of Consummation (Poemas de la consumación) *was published in 1968 when the poet was 70 years old. In it he returns to the subtle elliptical technique of his early surreal works with new perspective and maturity. He reviews the stages of human growth in terse, simple lines. Surreal images are made clearer as they are juxtaposed with insightful observations which are at times aphoristic: "To know is to laugh," "To live is not to sigh or to foresee words which may still live in us," "To live much is a dark way, and suddenly to know is not to know oneself," "Whoever is is a sign, / an image of one who thought . . ." In the last poem, "Forgetting" ("El olvido"), he says that "to remember is obscene; / worse: it is sad," while affirming paradoxically that "to forget is to die." These statements succinctly express a view of the inevitability and pervasiveness of human suffering that runs throughout Aleixandre's work. Yet the person he describes in this last poem dies "with dignity." While Aleixandre makes us aware of pain, he also conveys the possibility of nobility. He has said that all his poetry is "a longing for the light."*

Willis Barnstone
David Garrison

Poet's Preface

I would like to send a greeting to the English-speaking readers of this book but my eyes scarcely permit me to do so. They do allow me to state that everything which follows—a sampling of what I have attempted throughout my life—is only a question that one man asks other men. For poetry is not as much an answer to the world as it is a question which the world receives and hears from the lips of one who contemplates it. The answer does not belong to the poet but rather to one who hears his words if they reach their true destination. When I was young I felt the urge—I cannot be sure whether it was a frenetic or very mild urge—to investigate, to demand, to request, that is, to know. To be acquainted with something is not the same as to know it. The way to such acquaintance is life itself as we live it, and knowing—the closure of the dialogue of familiarity—comes only with death. As long as the poet lives he stretches out his hand, not with the significance of a paper offered to the world, but with the burning hope of a sympathetic heart. Where is that heart? Only and purely (if he finds it at all) in the reality of the reader. And this reading of the burning paper is the answer given to the primary enthusiasm of the poet, which is nothing less than to bring life back into the being of one who hears him.

To the readers of this book, spread throughout the precincts of another language, I send my question, and I hope—I cannot say it modestly—that it will be silently felt by whoever holds it in his or her hands. Whether there be one or many readers, one is everyone. The poet will quietly have received the total answer.

Adolescence

As if you came and went away quietly,
from another road
to another road. To see you,
and then again not to see you.
To cross over one bridge to another bridge.
— The quick step,
the vanquished happy light.

The boy I would be, looking
downstream at the waters,
and your passage in the mirror
flowing, disappearing.

D.G.

My Voice

I was born one summer night
between two pauses. Speak to me: I hear you.
I was born. If only you could see what agony
is in the easy moon.
I was born. Your name was joy;
under a radiance a hope, a bird.
Arriving, arriving. The sea was a throb,
the hollow of a hand, a lukewarm medal.
And now lights are finally possible: caresses, flesh,
        horizon,
meaningless talk
turning like ears, snails,
like an open lobe that wakens
(listen, listen!) in the trampled light.

W.B.

Now It is Late

If only I came like cautious silence.
(I don't know who used to say it.)
Under a moon of mother-of-pearl or fire,
under the huge flame or in the depths of coldness,
in that profound eye looking out
to avoid lips on fire.
I want to be right, I want to say that always,
on the mountain on a cross I sell my life,
I sell a risk begging their glances,
not knowing the rose will always die.

W.B. and D.G.

Silence

Under the sigh an unwatered garden.
O birds, the songs, the feathers.
This lyric blue hand never sleeping.
Lips the size of a bird. I'm not listening.
The landscape is laughter. Two waists making love.
Trees in shadow secrete voices. Silence.
So I go back to fog or hard silver,
on the lyric forehead I kiss water alone,
water from snow, heart or urn,
prophecy of kisses, (O they fit!),
where just now my ears didn't hear
the footsteps in the sand, or light or shadow.

D.G.

Love Poem

I love you, dream of the wind.
You merge with my fingers, are forgotten by the north
on delicate mornings of the world upside down
when it is easy to smile because the rain is soft.

It is delicious to ride in the heart of the river.
O fish friends, tell me the secret of your open eyes,
of my gazing that will flow into the sea,
holding up the keels of distant ships.

I love you, world voyagers, you who sleep
       on the water,
men who go to the Americas after clothing,
those who leave their aching nakedness on the beach
and draw a moonray across the shipdecks.

To journey hoping is a smile, is beautiful,
silver and gold have not changed their depths,
they toss on the waves, over the fishfins,
creating music or dream for the blondest hair.

Along the river bottom my desire departs
from innumerable villages that I held on my fingertips,
those darknesses—I was dressed in black—that I left
far away, etched on shoulders.

Hope is the earth, a cheek,
an immense eyelid where I know I exist.
Do you remember? In this world I was born one night
when adding and subtracting were the key to dreams.

Fish, trees, stones, hearts, medals,
over your concentric waves, yes, halted,
I move and, circling, seek myself, O center, O center,
road, voyagers of the world, of the future existing
beyond the seas, in my pulse-beat.

W.B.

Always

I am alone. Waves. Beach, hear me.
Out there dolphins or a sword.
The certainty of always, the no limits.
This tender unyellow head,
this stone of sobbing flesh . . .
Sand, sand, your clamor is mine.
Because of my shadow you are not like a breast.
Don't pretend that sails, that a breeze,
that a north wind, that a frenzied gale
will push your smile into the foam,
stealing ships from its blood.

Love, love, hold back your impure step.

W.B.

Instant

Look in my eyes. They conquer sound.
Listen to my grief like a moon.
So silver swirling on your throat
is sleeping or aching.
                    Or unknown.
                              Or dissolves.

Form. Clamor. O, hush. That's what I am.
I am thought or night held in.

Under your skin a dream doesn't advance,
a suspended landscape of fallow deer.

                    W.B. and D.G.

Whiteness

You the thorn, the white hearing.
World, world,
immensity of sky, heat, faraway storms.
Universe touched by a fingertip,
where an open wound
was yesterday a bee, today a rose, yesterday the inseparable.
I am you whirling among other veils,
silence or brightness, earth or stars;
I'm you myself, I, I'm you, mine,
between a flight of worlds under the cold,
shivering in the untalking whiteness,
separated from me like a knife
that separates two roses when it snows.

W.B. and D.G.

Suspended Heart

Bird like moon,
moon hanging or beautiful,
as low as a tightened heart,
suspended without thread from a dark tear.

That contagious sadness
down in the desolation of the void,
without a very handsome body,
without a soul or crystal
against which to bend a lovely ray.

The whiteness of the chest or perhaps the world,
the medallion hanging in the middle,
that kiss fixed in pure blood,
dolorous muscle, heart held still.

A lone bird—perhaps a shadow,
perhaps pulsing sorrowfully,
the edge of that beak which on some lip
cut some flowers, a yellow stamen or a pollen moon.

For those cold rays,
loneliness or realized medallion,
an almost tangible ghost
of a moon or of blood or a kiss at the end.

W.B. and D.G.

To Death

You come and go nimble like the sea,
never happy body,
cheerful shadow that escapes like the air,
almost all feather, floating the birds.

Joyful heart warmed in this winter night,
in this generous tall space in which you have wings,
in which long lips almost touch opposite horizons
like a long smile or a sudden huge bird.

You come and go like the slender cape,
like the remembrance of night escaping,
like the murmur of day being born now
here between my two lips or in my teeth.

Your generous body, roaring water,
water which falls like a young cascade,
water so easy to drink at daybreak
when all the stars are felt in living hands.

To comb the froth or the shadow,
no, to comb the sensual presence,
the edge of delirium in the dawn,
the sound of your life breathing.

To love, love. Of those who were born, who doesn't love?
Who is ignorant of the heart's borders,
its form, tangible to the hands,
to the recondite kisses when one never weeps?

Your generous body wraps around me,
young vine or growing light,
water stained by its nascent confine,
a kiss arriving with its name of kiss.

Your generous body which doesn't flee,
which is quietly spread out like the shadow,
like that humble gaze of a flesh
which is almost all vanquished eyelid.

All is carpet or lawn, or love or punishment.
To love you this way like the nearly green ground
which a warm wind quietly curves,
wind in the form of this chest
breathing over you when I weep.

W.B. and D.G.

Cobra

The cobra all eyes,
a mass lying down afternoon (low, cloud),
a mass among dry leaves
surrounded by hearts suddenly stopped.

Watches like throbbing
in the peaceful trees are birds with drooping necks,
friendly kisses for the base cobra
whose skin is silky or cold or sterile.

Cobra on crystal
hissing like the fresh knife that undoes a virgin,
morning fruit
whose velvet still forms a bird in the wind.

Girls like lagoons,
eyes like hopes,
nudes like leaves,
the cobra slithers lascivious, gazing at its other sky.

It crisscrosses the world,
a chain of bodies or bloods that touch each other
when the whole skin has fled like an eagle
concealing the sun. O cobra, love, love!

Love masses or ships or groans,
everything slowly, body to body,
between thighs of coldness or between breasts
the size of mounds of packed ice.

Lips, teeth or flowers, great snowfalls;
the land below convulses as it emerges.
Love the bottom with blood where the perfect
garnet glistens.

                              The world quivers.

             W.B. and D.G.

Inhuman World

A sea. A moon.
An hourless void under a sky flown away.
A clamor which escapes unmindful of the blood.
A light in the west, agile as the air.

Everything flies without limits on the road east,
on the road of the swift winds toward the core.
Where there are no birds, misleading clouds
whirl like foam of a total ocean.

There, there among the bright joys
of that blue, unknown to mortal men,
an ocean stirs that isn't blood,
a water that is not an anvil,
a green or giddiness
of something that rises finally with its spacious wings.

There man does not exist.
High eagles graze its inhuman edge.
Warm feathers elude the empty claws,
and a spiralling sun alone in the distance sends
gold waves, but never into our wrists.

The light, the gold, the song of subtleties.
A branch or fire ascends like an arm of roses.
A hand doesn't exist, but it would circle the sky,
searching blindly for the surge of crimson.

Huge air. Not a single voice yells out.
Depth without night where life is life.
Where death slips away like finite death,
with a fist shouting at the dry walls.

No!
Man is remote. High wall of blood.
Man deafly screams out his forest heart.
His dripping blood, his stone sadness.
Covered by the shreds of a far crumbled
sky, man against a wall is drying up.

W.B. and D.G.

The Poet

For you who know how the stone sings,
and whose delicate pupil knows about the weight of mountains
         on a gentle eye,
and how one day the resounding clamor of forests easily drifts
         into sleep through our veins;

for you, poet, who felt in your courage
the brutal attack of celestial birds,
and in whose words powerful eagle wings
         fly as quickly
as flashing loins of warm soundless fish:

hear this book I place in your hands
with forest air,
but where suddenly a drop of freshest dew flares on a rose,
or cosmic desire is pulsating,
where sorrow like a hurt eyelid
closes the day and hides the sun like a darkened tear,
while the huge weary forehead
feels an unlit kiss, a long kiss,
a few mute words spoken by the dying world.

Yes, poet: love and grief are your kingdom.
Your mortal flesh, warm with spirit,
burns at night or ascends at powerful noon,
an immense prophetic tongue licking the heavens,
infusing words with light and killing men.

The youth of your heart is not a beach
where the sea attacks with scattered foam:
love's teeth that chew borders of land
and roar quietly to its creatures.

It is not the alert lightning, abrupt and menacing,
flashing on your naked face
to sink into your eyes and ignite you, igniting
space with your life, burning away with love.

No. That light in the world,
not its last ash,
that light which never fails like dust on lips,
is you, poet, whose hand and no moon
I saw one night shining in the heavens.

A strong chest lolling, pierced by the sea,
breathes like the celestial tide
and opens its recumbent arms touching
the extreme rims of the earth.

And then?
Yes, poet. Throw away this book which tries to hold a sunflash
        in its pages,
and look face to face at light, your head against
        a rock,
while your remote feet feel the last kiss of twilight
and your raised hands fondle the moon,
and your tossing hair is a path among the stars.

W.B. and D.G.

The Body and the Soul

But it is sadder, much sadder.
Sad like the branch that drops its fruit for no one.
Even sadder. Like that vapor
the dead pulp sprays from the earth.
Like a hand rising from a supine body
wanting only to hug lights,
the pained smile, the soundless velvet night.
Evening light on the body stretched out and soulless.
Soul outside, the body's soul floating
delicately above the sad abandoned form.
Soul of tiny mist hanging
over yesterday's lover, vulnerable body,
chill, pale with the nocturnal hours
and still, alone, subdued, empty.

The soul of love sees and moves apart,
cautious, and at last withdraws tenderly cold.

W.B. and D.G.

You Almost Loved Me

"Heavenly soul born to love."
Espronceda

You almost loved me.
You used to smile, with your mass of blond hair where the
        sunlight slips handsomely.
Before your hands the brilliancy of day became evenly mellow,
giving distance to your perfect body.
The playful transparency of light did not offend;
it lay gold around your unhurt brightness.
Almost, you almost loved me.

I was coming from there, from beyond, from that dark
        consciousness
of earth, from a shadowy green growth of exhausted forests
where the wind grew too old for red melodies,
where no flowers opened celestially in the mornings,
no arc of birds at dawn found the day virgin.

An ocean depth surrounded you.
An unbroken mother-of-pearl shell beneath your foot
tenders you like the last drop of seafoam.
Almost, you almost loved me.

Why did you turn your eyes away, virgin from the core
        of the world?
This spring afternoon
you place moon coldness over daylight
and like a disc of nightless chastity
race roseate through inviolate blue.

Your lovely oblique face—a pensive rose without destiny—
stares at the sea. Why, why are you deaf,
and with your long hair swelling in the wind,
why deny the rays of your lunar beauty?

But you loved me like the light! Don't escape,
dull, insensitive, dusky, sealed.
Almost, you almost loved me. On the pure waves
of the sea I felt your body like starry foam,
warm, alive, propagative. No, no, the kiss
wasn't born of light: aristocratic
words rang out: you promised me the hidden
world, I kissed your breath, while the arched wave
broke over my lips, and like a beach I had
the full warmth of your beauty in my arms.

Yes, yes, you loved me on the brilliant surfaces, steady,
final, ecstatic. The unmoving sea
held its permanent breath
and I saw the moon blaze in the skies,
happy, kissed, and reveal the world to me.

W.B. and D.G.

The Immortals

I
Rain

The waist is not a rose.
Not a bird. Not feathers.
The waist is the rain,
fragility, a moan
giving itself to you. Use
your mortal arm to hug
fresh water, a love
complaint. Embrace, embrace it!
The entire rain looks like
a single reed. How it wavers
if there is wind, if your mortal arm
is there, yes, today, you who love it!

II
Sun

Light, almost weightless:
the sandal. Footsteps
with no flesh. Solitary goddess,
from a world she demands walking space
for her body high
and solar. Don't say long
hair; burning hair.
Say sandal, light
footstep; don't say
earth, but fresh grass
crackling in that flash,
so soft that it loves her
when she walks on it. O feel
your light, your grave solar
touch! Here, feeling you,
the earth is sky. And shines.

III
Word

One day the word was
heat: a human lip.
It was the light of young morning; more: lightning
in this naked eternity. Someone
loved. With no before or after. And the logos
was born. Word alone and pure
forever—Love—in beautiful space!

IV
Earth

Deeply moved, the earth
exhales its vegetable
joy. Look: it is born!
Green blush, today it sails
through a still new space.
What does it enclose? Alone, pure in
itself, no one inhabits it.
Only the mute primigenial
grace of the earth
moves in stars—airy, virgin—
in the gold light.

V
Fire

The whole fire dangles
passion. Light alone!
Look how pure it ascends
till it licks the skies,
while all the birds
fly through it. It doesn't burn!
And man? Never. That fire
is still
free of you.
It is light, innocent light.
Human beings, never be born!

VI
Air

Even more than the sea, the air—
huger than the sea—is calm.
High unpeopled vigil of lucidity.
Perhaps one day the crust of the earth
could feel you, human. But the unconquered
air doesn't know it lived in your chest.
No memory, deathless, the air glitters.

VII
Sea

Who said perhaps that the sea moans
sadly, lip of love, toward the beaches?
Let it spread out enveloped in light.
Glory, glory on high, and on the sea, gold!
Ah, sovereign light that envelops, sings
the imperishable age of the sensual sea!
There, reverberating
timeless, the sea exists.
Heart of a deathless god, throbbing!

W.B. and D.G.

My Father (fragment)

for my sister

Father, you are remote in your kingdom of shade.
Look at your son, dark in this orphan twilight,
far from the benevolent light of your constant eyes.
There I was born and grew; from that pure light
I took life, and that serene glow
was drawn into this form, which still says farewell,
like an unheard echo, to your dazzling light.

W.B. and D.G.

Epitaph

To obliterate your name,
fiery body waiting in the earth
like a god for oblivion, here I name you,
edge of a life; here, precise
body that once burned. No tomb: free earth.

Put away the slow look
that a harsh rock might reclaim from you
or that a tree without its birds demands
(chaste in the night, in its vigil naked).

Never let river noise be heard.
Deep in the earth the dead man lives
as absolute earth.
                    Pass by,
your steps will echo in no other chest.

W.B. and D.G.

To Fray Luis de León

What slender brook—a daughter and a tomb
derived from hills of ice—explodes in chills,
pours waters over silent mounds, and spills
out firmaments, speeds radiance into gloom?

What mute orchestral water in the brume
of gently jealous air fuses the frills
of crackling foam in soaring copies. Fills
smooth dialogue so sign and radiance bloom

as twins? Tall night submits its famous tree—
a massive top—raising it to clean skies:
its growth and handsome branches huge throughout.

A youthful breeze from heaven eagerly
opens, and—spreading out its pomp—there lies
in place, slowly in place, and stars ring out.

W.B.

To Don Luis de Góngora

O what firm construct raises high its beam
out of the landscape, urgent, wild with beauty,
but shaped to penetrate the certainty
of air, supplanting it with bold new scheme?

Lines gravely slanting go. But from its base
the curve stems upward in an arched perfection
around the top, and leaves the bark protection
whole, capturing a world of pomp and grace.

The sky disperses meditated light
in subtle rhythms of the western wind
and lofty currents answer its command.

Without the rainbow, hidden hues incite
the airy mansions where they vibrate, pinned,
and ring out perfect harmony's demand.

D.G.

Final Shadow

All thought is gone, a soul of shadow looms.
Who are you here I slowly kiss alone?
A soul or unlit shape or lethal bone
unmoving, which my fever now consumes?

Here our blind passion blew up and was chill.
Here my heart pounded furiously obsessed,
insisted stubbornly, throbbing oppressed.
Here my mouth lost its ecstasy. And still

I took you blind into my arms, held you
lover under my chest where you breathed eas-
ily. In you, my blood lived its vibration.

O dark night! Now I have no hope. I'm through.
Loneliness tells no lie to my sensation,
and now pure shadow reigns in utter peace.

W.B.

In the Square

It's beautiful, beautifully humble and trusting, exhilarating
      and profound,
to feel yourself under the sun with others, pushed,
jostled, pulled, mingled, swept clamorously along.

No good
to stay on shore
like the pier or the shellfish that only wants to calcify
      in imitation of a rock.
But how pure and serene to obliterate yourself in the joy
      of being lost in the tide,
to find yourself in the movement with which the great heart
      of men pulsates expanded.

Like someone who lives over there—I don't know on which floor;
I've seen him go down the stairs
and merge courageously in the multitude and lose himself.
The great throng poured by. But his tiny heart was seen afloat.
Who would recognize him? There, with hope, resolve or faith,
      with timid boldness,
with quiet modesty, he too
was stirring.

It was a great open square and it had the smell of existence.
A smell of great uncovered sun and of the wind curling it,
a huge wind running its hand over heads,
its great hand that grazed the foreheads joined together,
      reassured them.

And it was the meandering that moved
like a unique being; I don't know if it was helpless or powerful,
but it was alive and perceptible, it covered the earth.

There everyone can see himself and be happy and know himself.
When—in the melting afternoon, alone in your study,
with strange eyes and a question in your mouth—
you'd like to ask something of your image,

don't seek yourself in the mirror,
in an extinct dialogue where you don't hear yourself.
Go down, go down slowly and look for yourself among others.
Everyone is there and you're among them.
Go naked, fuse and know yourself.

Go in slowly, like the timid bather who, with much love and
      fear of the water,
first slips his feet into the foam
and feels the water surge around him, then dares, then almost decides.

And now, with water at his waist, he's still not certain.
But he stretches his arms, opens his two arms and surrenders
      completely.
And there sees himself strong and straightens up and lunges
ahead splashing up foam and dives and is certain,
and slices through, throbbing in the living waters and sings and
      is young.

Go in with naked feet. Go into the seething, into the
      square.
Go into the redeeming torrent and be yourself.
O small diminutive heart, heart longing to beat
and be the concordant heart coming near.

D.G.

The Dream

There are moments of loneliness
when the heart knows dumbly that it doesn't love.
We have just sat up in bed, tired: the dark day.
Someone is still sleeping innocent on that bed.
But perhaps we are asleep . . . Ah, no: we move.
And we are sad, hushed. Outside, the insistent rain.
Morning of slow merciless mist. So alone!
We look through the windowpanes. Clothes fallen down,
stifling air, noisy water. And the room
freezing in this hard winter which is somehow different outside.

And you keep quiet, your face in your hand.
Your elbow on the table. The chair silent.
And the only sound is someone's slow breathing,
that woman over there, serene, beautiful, sleeping
and dreaming that you don't love her, and you are her dream.

W.B. and D.G.

The Mirror

I

I look at you in the mirror.
I row through lights, I search
for your flesh, O my dream,
image rejecting
a truth. I move forward
through impalpable, harsh
waters: only lights.
How sad my body is
in your mist! How cold
its wing flaps in your depth!
O eternal voyager
escaping into glass!

II

But I know that alone,
happy, there in the depths
of the tenebrous and still
mirror, there, explored,
happy, my body
rests. O still glass,
tricky,
you defend me. I know
what you keep in your chasm
and I am happy. Go on
lying, let your
warped glass, your foam
of light — O surface —
be just illusion . . .

(The thin glass says nothing.)

W.B. and D.G.

My Night

Homage
to Saint John of the Cross

The whole night is sealed,
dizzy. Hazy burnished
walls. Fixed stars
tumble awkwardly.
The seamless night
is a dead fallen bell.
The live voice of tall night
is extinguished on earth.
Paralyzed fields. Night, night,
don't lie. Dumb, cold,
you whirl, toll unspeaking
and spin soundlessly.

Everything is a sign. Slowly
until halted,
the night persists. Chasms.
Light and shadow. Planes. Life.
The soul no longer feels itself.
It feels everything. Unheard
passion. Tell me, will dying
make the night mine?
Then let me die. Night,
dying I feel you. Sacred
reality! You are heard. You
are. My life is mine.

W.B. and D.G.

The Years

Are the years his burden or his history?
What hurts most is leaving
slowly, still full of love, smiling. And they say, "Young,
ah, how young you look." Look, not are? The phrase is precise.
Surprising people go by. His eye—which is still lively—stares
and copies gold of hair, pink flesh, whiteness of sudden ivory. And
laughter is bright
for everyone and for him, and he's alive and hears it.
But the years spill out
a kind of round troubled clarity,
and he keeps walking into the hated beacon—not visible
or barely so, for it goes by unknown, disguised.

The round glass or air cannot
be broken: that unending cone harboring something,
a being that still moves about and is by now invisible.
While others free, cruise about, blinding.

And blinding us they give off life in fresh rays.
But he who goes out alone, safely hooded
by age, slips by unheard. The air is frozen.
He hears and feels, for the strange wall
robs him of light, but it is only air
for the coming light which slips inside.
His soul is pierced, he is living, on his feet,
     and still cruising about.

W.B.

Vision of Youth from Other Years

At birth words
are squandered saying death, terror.
As when between two sounds there is a kiss or a whisper.
To know is to laugh, and the dawn laughs.

It laughs, for the earth is a human chest beating convulsively.
A full laughter that isn't sound but life,
but lights exhaled by
something, a chest: the planet.

It is a joyful body.
What is on it doesn't matter.
Only its mammoth quivering in space.
Like a floating, happy child.
So the youth looked and saw the world, free.

Maybe between two kisses,
maybe at the heart of a kiss:
that's what he felt between two lips.
It was fresh laughter, his or the world's.

But the world endures,
not just between two lips: the kiss ends.
But the rolling world,
free, yes, is like a kiss
even after it dies.

W.B. and D.G.

A Few Words

I would say
a few words in your ear. An indecisive man has little
> *faith.*
To live much is a dark way, and suddenly to know
> *is not to know oneself.*
But even so I would talk. For my eyes repeat
> *what they copy:*
your beauty, your name, the river sound, the forest,
> *the soul by itself.*

He saw it all and they have it. That's what the eyes say.
They respond to whoever sees them. But they never
> *ask.*
Because if they keep on taking
color from light, mud from gold,
and clear dregs from every taste,
then they must know kisses, noises, smells,
and have seen great trees, silent
> *whispers,*
dead bonfires, embers, veins, ash,
and the sea, down to its floor, with its slow
> *thorns,*
remains of lovely bodies that beaches wash up.

A few words, while someone keeps still:
wind in the leaves as I kiss
> *your lips.*
Some bright words as I sleep in your lap.
Water humming on the stones. Meanwhile,
> *quiet, I am dead.*

W.B. and D.G.

At Last

One more word, and it sounded imprecise.
An echo sometimes like sudden song.
Or else it caught fire like tinder.
At times it had the sound of great trees
        in the darkness.
The beating of huge wings: eagles, ascents,
        palpitations, thrones.
Then higher wings, lights.

More lights or flashing shadow.
The scattered sound and silence of the world.
Desolation
of the rimless void.

And abruptly the last word:
water caressing a thirsty mouth,
or the tender drop on blind eyes
burned by life and its fires.

Ah, what peace: sleep.

                        W.B. and D.G.

Doesn't Know

Youth doesn't know, that's why it goes on, endures.
Where are you going? And the wind blows, pushes
the runners who almost spin and go, go with the wind,
graceful on the sea: foot over foam.

Life. Life is to be young and nothing else. Listen,
listen . . . But the hushed sound
doesn't betray itself
except on the lips of the young.
They hear it in the kiss. Only they,
with their sharp hearing
catch it, or listen.
Red kissed swelling flesh which they enunciate.

D.G.

Limits and Mirror

Don't insist. Youth doesn't deceive. It shines alone.
In a naked chest the day is dying.
It is not the words that fool me.
But the pure silence being born here.
At your borders. The quiet outline limits you.
But it doesn't diminish you. Your truth throbbing here
    in space!

II

Only a naked body shows borders.
Whoever limits himself is. You on the earth.
How differently earth expands
and draws together and shines and, finally, takes fire,
flesh or resin, or lofty body shivering
with fire. O if to live is to burn, then die!

III

But whoever dies is born, and here you still exist.
The same woman? A face is not a mirror though
    it repeats
her expression. Perhaps her voice. In the mirror an image
    of a sound
freezes. On the glass her lip left imprints!
Only the vapor of what you loved.

D.G.

Face Behind the Glass
(The Old Man's Gaze)

Late or soon or never.
But there behind the glass the face persists.
Next to some natural flowers the flower itself appears
in the form of color, cheek, rose.
Behind the glass the rose is always a rose,
but doesn't smell.
Distant youth is precisely that.
But here it can't be heard.

Only light pierces the virgin glass.

D.G.

You Wait

A city in the depths waits for a wind.
You walk in it. Whoever sees is fooled,
whoever doesn't look understands.
To look long was the light: your eyes, blind.
Hush. The shadow moves on. It's the sleeping city in still
        deeper sleep.
Nocturnal dust, and eyes,
eyes in that dark mist. Above, night.
Hush. Solitude lying down is also sleeping.
Alone, naked,
you wait.

W.B. and D.G.

Raining

Raining this afternoon and your image
rains purely. The day opens up in my memory.
      You came in.
I don't hear. Memory gives me only your image.
Only your kiss or rain falls into my remembrance.
Your voice rains, and a sad kiss rains,
a profound kiss,
kiss drenched with rain. Moist lip.
Moist with memory the kiss cries
from gray delicate
skies.
Your love rains wetting my memory
and falls and falls. A kiss
falls into depth. And gray rain, still gray,
is falling.

           W.B.

The Poet Remembers His Life

> "To die, to sleep; to sleep:
> perchance to dream." —*Hamlet*

Forgive me: I was asleep.
And to sleep is not to live. Peace to men.
To live is not to sigh or to foresee words which
     may still live in us.
Do we live in them? Words die.
They ring beautifully but never last.
Like this bright night. Yesterday when the dawn,
or when the completed day extends its last
ray, and perhaps it strikes your face.
With a sable brush of light it closes your eyes.
Sleep:
the night is long, but now it is over.

W.B. and D.G.

Night Cave

Look at it. Here kissing you, I say it. Look at it.
In this dark cave, look, look
at my kiss, my final darkness that in definitive
night
cloaks your luminous daybreak
splitting
blackness, and like sun in me informs me
of other truth. Which you, profound, don't know.
From your being all my brightness comes to me
from you, my funereal daybreak opening in the evening.
You, my nocturnity, you blind me, light.

W.B.

Yesterday

That curtain of yellow silks
which a sun still turns into gold and a sigh ripples.
The past rolls in the wind and crackles.
It is still in space, but is thought
or seen. Sleeping, whoever looks at it says nothing,
sees a silence, or it's a love asleep.

To sleep, to live, to die. Slowly the silk cracks, minute,
delicate, dreamt: real. Whoever is is a sign,
an image of one who thought, and here it is.
It weaves where life warped slowly, and thread by thread
held on. It halts the breath in which it still is moving.

Not to know is to live. To know is to die away.

W.B. and D.G.

Posthumous Kiss

Although silenced, my lips are still in yours,
I breathe you. O dream in life, or there is life.
The suspect life is in the kiss
alive by itself. Without us, it shines.
We are its shadow. Because it is our body when
we are not.

W.B.

The Limit

Enough. It's no abuse to look at the long brilliance
of your eyes. There, to the end of the world.
I looked and received. I contemplated, and went away.
The dignity of man is in his death.
But temporal brilliancies bring
color, truth. The meditated light fools us.
Enough. In the fullness of light — your eyes — I placed
my faith. Through them I saw, lived perhaps.
Today as I walk near my ending, I kiss these borders.
You, my limitation, my dream. Be!

W.B. and D.G.

Impure Dream

Vain truth of a still insistent body.
Black eyes. More light. Crystals. Gleam.
When sunset sinks into night one can
be unaware of other eyes. Black ones are night, and like
  night they blind.
But night is nothing: a dream, impure ·
for there's a live breath still at its edges.
The tenebrous waves are calling.
I see nothing, know nothing. The dawn, or never.

D.G.

Permanence

Too sad to say it.
The trees deceive. While in brightness
        only the waters go by.
Only the land is firm.

But flesh is dream
if it is seen, nightmare if it is felt.
Vision if one flees it.
Stone if one dreams it.

Be still by the rock, and sleep.

                        D.G.

Another Truth

The volubility
of the wind announces
another
truth. I still hear, and never,
that inaudible whistling
in the penumbra.
O be still:
listen.
But the lip is quiet
and doesn't modulate
that mysterious sound I hear
at the level of the kiss. Glow,
let your lip glow its warmth or rays
of the sun that startle the unspeaking lip,
like another blind mouth.
Ah impure thirst
for light, thirst live or dead, in the final
mouth.

W.B. and D.G.

Forgetting

Your end is not an empty cup
that must be drained. Throw away the shell and die.

So in your hand you slowly lift
a flash or its mention, and your fingers burn
like sudden snow.
It is here and was not, but it was and makes no sound.
The cold burns and in your eyes his memory
is born. To remember is obscene;
worse: it is sad. To forget is to die.

He died with dignity. His shadow passes on.

D.G.

Aliki

The times I saw her she came enveloped
among her brothers. She was little
and in the room where we were
(while I was speaking to her parents)
the three children looked at me
as at a mountain or a green hill
and with happy shouting they climbed,
        they mounted, they surmounted me.
Aliki was the big little one.
Gracefully she ascended on one flank,
first reaching a knee, then climbing to my chest
where she rested a moment;
        then with new Alpine drive
she shimmied up to a shoulder and there,
as if what she described from that height
        were the universe,
she extended her gaze all about
and, bending her arm over the peak,
rested her small head in her hand
and there remained ultimate, supreme on the mountain
summit.

The boys marauded at my feet, through the valley,
climbed the first escarpments. But she, only she,
queenly at the summit, seemed almost asleep,
thoughtful, seated gracefully on my shoulder.

The three children got together, excited, romping
over each other. But at times Aliki
suddenly drew apart. How often I saw her,
with her colored pencils, in one corner
of the room, drawing minutely something

that could have been the birth of the world,
from its original pupil, in its timeless
dawn.

Today I do not see her but I feel her.
Aliki has shot up, her childhood has grown.
Her eyes are bright, with an unstained clarity;
her cheek has received the intact passage
of light and on her small teeth a splendor
has spread, unpausing, as for a whole day,
a splendor that is unrelenting.

What breeze has moved her childhood hair?
What trembling has blown about her moonless forehead?
Where did the brilliant light come from
that has reached her and cannot be ephemeral?

Aliki lift your hand, open it. Where do you
come from?

And there, great, immense, against the horizon,
I see her raise her arm and trap impossible birds,
surprise blinking stars, catch summers, steppes,
furies, sounds, tiny colored butterflies
or simply the intact aroma of the world.

Because here she is, innocent, mysterious,
profound.

W.B.

About the Poet

Although Vicente Aleixandre was born in Seville, his early youth was spent in Málaga, on the southern Mediterranean coast of Spain. In 1909 his family moved to Madrid. He studied and later taught law and business administration, then worked a few years for a railway company until illness forced him to quit his job and convalesce in the mountains. From then on he dedicated himself to his writing and soon began to publish books. One of his early ones, La destrucción o el amor, *gained him the National Prize for Literature. Another illness kept him in Spain during the Spanish Civil War (1936-39). He was one of few prominent Spanish writers who survived that war in his native country; most died or went into temporary or permanent exile.*

Aleixandre has always been a friend, model and source of encouragement to other poets. In 1949 he became a member of the Spanish Royal Academy, in 1963 and 1969 he received the Critics Award, and in 1977 he won the Nobel Prize. He lives on the outskirts of Madrid on a street which has been renamed in his honor—La Calle de Vicente Aleixandre.

About the Translators

Willis Barnstone, poet and critic, is the author of several books of poems, including From This White Island *(Twayne),* A Day in the Country *(Harper & Row), and* China Poems *(University of Missouri). His anthology* Modern European Poetry *(Bantam) includes major European poets translated by American and British poets. He is also the translator of volumes of poems by Sappho, Saint John of the Cross, Fray Luis de León, Pedro Salinas, and Antonio Machado. A Guggenheim Fellow and recipient of both the Cecil Hemley and Lucille Medwick awards from the Poetry Society of America, he is Professor of Comparative Literature at Indiana University.*

David Garrison has published articles on Spanish writers including Cervantes, Góngora and Aleixandre. His translations, reviews and original poems have appeared in various magazines and anthologies. He is Associate Professor of Spanish and Portuguese at Wright State University in Dayton, Ohio.

About the Spanish Texts and the Translations

The poems of Vicente Aleixandre have been translated from his Obras completas, *Volume I (1924-1967) and Volume II (1965-1973), Madrid: Aguilar, copyrights 1968 and 1978.*

Translations in this anthology have previously appeared in:
The Nation, Mundus Artium, Denver Quarterly, Chicago Review, Modern Poetry in Translation, Lotus, Cutbank, Hispanic Arts,
and also in:
Willis Barnstone, ed., Modern European Poetry *(New York: Bantam, 1950) Lewis Hyde, ed.,* A Longing for the Light: Selected Poems of Vicente Aleixandre *(New York: Harper and Row. 1979).*

"Raining" received the Chicago Review *annual award in 1979 for its best published poem of the year.*